The **Fiona Harrold** Coaching Series

Get
Motivated

Mike Blissett

7 Steps to the life you want

HODDER
MOBIUS

Copyright © 2005 by Mike Blissett

First published in Great Britain in 2005 by Hodder and Stoughton
A division of Hodder Headline

The right of Mike Blissett to be identified as the Author
of the Work has been asserted by him in accordance with the
Copyright, Designs and Patents Act 1988.

A Mobius Book

10 9 8 7 6 5 4 3 2 1

A CIP catalogue record for this title is
available from the British Library

ISBN 0 340 83702 0

Typeset in Stone Serif by Palimpsest Book Production Limited,
Polmont, Stirlingshire
Printed and bound by Clays Ltd, St Ives plc

Hodder Headline's policy is to use papers that are natural,
renewable and recyclable products and made from wood grown in
sustainable forests. The logging and manufacturing processes are expected
to conform to the environmental regulations of the country of origin.

Hodder and Stoughton Ltd
A division of Hodder Headline
338 Euston Road
London NW1 3BH

Contents

4 areas to work on.

Family, Friends, work
hobbies, leisure, time close,
personal growth, contribution
to the community, relationships

Acknowledgements

Thank you to Mum and Dad, Karen and Sue for your unconditional love and support all these years. To Joe, Emerson, and all my friends, you have all at some stage been my personal guru. To the whole team at Hodder and Stoughton and Helen in particular, for being the coolest editor there is and Sheila at AP Watt for connecting A with B and making this idea work. Much gratitude and respect to the many wonderful people I have had the good fortune to coach over the past few years; I salute you. And finally, to my good friend Fiona – simply, you made it all possible. With all my heart, thank you.

P21

P29

P30 wheel of life.

P32-31.

P35.

Foreword by Fiona Harrold

You are going to love this book! Mike's enthusiasm and commitment to you leap off every page and I can assure you, they are totally genuine. Mike is one of my personally chosen team of coaches whom I work with closely and I recommend and direct clients to him all the time. I see and hear the results of his work with people and I can honestly tell you, he helps people turn their lives around. I've seen him motivate the most resigned, downright dejected individuals and inspire them to shake up their lives, lose weight, gain confidence, increase their self-esteem and develop the guts to make life-changing decisions and take decisive action.

I believe you can only have this impact on another person when your desire to help is utterly genuine and your skill in doing so innately gifted. Mike has also spent many years studying and training to make himself the brilliant coach he is. I am delighted that he has written this book so that you can benefit from his support in the way that, up until now, only his private clients have. Use him as your personal coach. Suspend your disbelief and self-doubt and work with him on taking your life to its next level. Trust me when I say that if you step up and make the commitment, do the work, life will only get better. Strong motivation, right attitude and right action is the combination that we all need to achieve our dreams and ambitions. This is what you'll get here with Mike on these pages. Do the work. Follow his guidelines and get motivated. Take action and stay on track; get in touch and tell us about your progress through our website, www.fionaharrold.com

Good luck!

Fiona Harrold
London, 2005

1

What Do You Want?

To accomplish great things, we must not only act, but also dream; not only plan, but also believe

ANATOLE FRANCE

Why do some people simply coast through life, achieving and enjoying seemingly unlimited success, oblivious to failure, while others feel overwhelmed just at the thought of trying to create the life they always dreamed of? The answer lies in the planning, the doing, the getting up and going – in the direction that's right for you. By taking control and assuming responsibility for what you have, and don't have in life, you become a much more powerful and effective version of the person you currently are.

Ask yourself where you are now, and whether that is where you want to be. If it's not, this book is for you.

It's about putting a plan of action together that will become your route to success. To do that, you will need to assume total responsibility for your own destiny. How much control do you have over that right now? Eighty per cent? Fifty per cent? Lower? Only forty, twenty . . . And if you don't control your own life, then who does: your partner, family, friends, the government? What would it take for you to begin a process of taking back your own power, assuming full responsibility for your own destiny? Because that's what increased motivation and focus will give you: your independence!

In *Get Motivated – 7 Steps to the Life You Want* I'm going to help you to develop your personal game plan. By examining what you want, what motivates and moves you, your dreams, goals and ambitions – even the long-forgotten pipe dreams of childhood – you will be able to put together a step-by-step approach to creating the life you want.

'But how can I get motivated, so that my life works in a better way?' is probably the question I'm asked most frequently. As a coach, I believe that you, the client, already hold all the answers within. *Get Motivated* is a step-by-step approach to creating your ideal life – the one that works best for you. By taking responsibility for and being proactive about your life suddenly anything is possible. The goalposts move. We expand our horizons. With that in mind I invite you to suspend self-doubt for the duration and begin by believing that yes, you can create something wonderful. Life is indeed a 'work in progress'; look at it that way and anything is possible.

YOUR IDEAL LIFE

The first question to ask yourself seems obvious, and is: 'What do I want?' Sounds like an easy question, doesn't it? In fact when most people are asked what they want from life, what they want to create and to achieve, they reply with a long, animated description of their current life, or more often an even longer tale of what they don't want.

Why is that? Could it be we've become accustomed to such a steady diet of negativity that even when offered the possibility of a better life, we are so immune to a brighter side that we simply sabotage success? For most of us, from infancy, and with the best of intentions, our carers and teachers fed us negative, self-limiting beliefs, and as children we absorb everything as absolute gospel.

How many of the following limiting beliefs did you hear as children, and how many still exist in your life today?

- Be careful
- Don't be silly
- Don't daydream

- Don't talk/ be quiet
- Don't be stupid
- You're really naughty
- Stop it
- Stop doodling
- You're really scruffy

Tick the ones that ring bells with you, and over the next few days write down all the other limiting beliefs you picked up or heard through your childhood and teenage years. Then think honestly which ones are still part of your belief system today. How do they limit you? Write this down and give examples. Only by highlighting and seeing old, out-of-date beliefs for what they are, and what they cost us, will we ever be in a position to move forward from them.

Focus is so fundamentally important. For example, is it better to say, 'I know this meeting is going to be terrible', or 'I know this meeting is going to be a challenge, full of opportunity'? You decide. Do you see the cup as half full, or half empty? From now on I want you to see possibilities, not deficiencies.

What do you see as your ideal life? It is essential to be able to visualise it. Touch, feel, hear, smell and taste it, too, and you'll have a powerful catalyst to your dreams. Begin by writing at least a page of A4 about what this ideal life would look like. Where would you live? What would your ideal house look like? Would you live alone, or with somebody – if so, who (and get descriptive here too)? What would you do for career, fun, travel, hobbies, enjoyment? What would send you into hysterical laughter, or make you cry with happiness? Who would you love? So many questions; but then you are talking 'ideal life', and not something run of the mill and ordinary, aren't you?

This chapter is about refocusing on the infinite possibilities for living a better life that are staring you in the face, right at this very moment. Even people who when asked to describe their best life scenario say they haven't got a clue have more than a clue; they know exactly what they want. We all do. Maybe we gloss over it, bury our dream without trace for years at a time under tonnes of so-called reality. But that doesn't mean it's not there. It will always be there. No matter how long we ignore its existence, our dream remains. The worst that will happen is that we will have wasted valuable years. I don't want that to happen to you: I want you to focus on getting motivated to achieve your dreams right now.

Ask yourself: 'Who would I have to become in order to create my ideal life? Would I need to learn a new skill, upgrade or change my image, model myself on another person I perceive as having already attained the kind of life I want?'

Write down all your answers and, above all, keep them out and to hand for the foreseeable future. A plan filed away in a drawer or cabinet, no matter how beautiful and well written, is pointless unless it's being used.

I CAN DO THAT!

Can you? If I asked you what you are capable of doing, what would you say? I've heard all the self-limiting beliefs: 'Oh, I can't do anything, I'm not qualified, I only know how to do my present job, I have no experience.' Enough! I want you to list all the many skills I'm sure you have. Spend thirty minutes now, followed by fifteen minutes over each of the next few days and come up with at least fifty.

I, too, was challenged to do this years ago, and even though at first I had the same reaction as you, I was soon surprised with the list I produced. Once I began to free my mind of its 'thinking in the box' limitations, I soon came up with such diverse skills as:

- Being able to drive
- Writing short fiction and articles (travel, reviews)
- Using a computer
- Talking and liking to explain things to people
- Acting
- Singing
- Playing the guitar
- Showing friends around London when they visited
- Reading books, magazines and newspapers

What would the list look like for you? Remember, I'm not asking what you'd *like* to do, but what you *could* do.

> What you believe about yourself is the key to your future growth, the secret ingredient that will propel you to new heights, the foundation to whatever you want to achieve in life. Without strong and supportive beliefs the going will be tough, so it's vital that you clear your mind of negativity and hold on to the belief that change is possible

DREAM + FOCUS = REALITY

I know you have what it takes to succeed. The reason I know this is because you are reading this book right now. Simply by picking this up you have expressed a desire to succeed, to attain greater self-development and achieve more in your life. You are about to become super-motivated, a person who lives and breathes pizzazz and oomph.

I want you to believe that by working with me you will become so completely focused that the only move you can make is forward. Taking the next step in your life will be as easy as the last one – except that the next step will be the big one, the one that moves you in the direction of what you really want to achieve.

How far can you go? How big are your imagination,

your goals, your dreams? If I were to ask you to visualise the universe in your mind, what would you see? Would it be a huge, stagnant, empty place: a void? Or would you describe an ever expanding, always evolving dream factory of life and nature: fireworks, bangs, new galaxies, stars imploding, dying and being replaced by new, bigger, and even more fantastically beautiful ones? I think we both know your answer. How do I know? Partly because you're reading this in the first place, and partly because I have stood there, too: wanting to be inspired, taken on a voyage of self-discovery that would ultimately enable me to elevate my life. That is how I see you. Your potential is ruled only by the size of your imagination. You are amazing, a fantastic creature on the verge of an immense journey of discovery. I believe your potential is limitless. All I need from you is to believe the same.

HOW TO USE THIS BOOK

This book is based on principles of openness and self-development; it is designed to increase your awareness and open your mind to the vast potential life has to offer. Read it sequentially, from beginning to end, working through the tasks as they come up. Listen and absorb everything. Venture out and try the new techniques. Don't be overly concerned by failure, because, as you will learn, out of failure comes success. Be brave, be the very best you can be. Don't half do this, or half commit to moving forward. Make the decision. Do it now. This is your life; you need to value it as a prize. If you suffer a dip in motivation, have a down day, miss a few targets, don't beat yourself up – it's important to carry on. Just be thankful for the experience, pick yourself up and keep on moving.

Work through the tasks, and complete them with an open and inquisitive mind; embrace the new you I know you want to create. Learn from and appreciate other people's experiences. You may identify with them or just be thankful that you avoided that particular stage of the journey yourself. We all have our roads to travel – the point is to believe that we do the driving ourselves. We can make a difference to our own lives whenever we desire, whatever age we might be; we can design the life we want. Take my word for it now, at the beginning of this book, and believe it for yourself by the end! All the work we do from here on is designed to open up your options, begin to focus and home in on what you really want, then go ahead and get it.

'What we sow, so shall we reap.' This basic belief of so many eastern faiths is, I believe, one of the guiding forces of the universe. If our beliefs control our actions, then it would also follow that a sad, distrustful, negative mindset would attract sad, distrustful and negative energy towards us. Consequently, if we focus on a vibrant, happy, positive life then we will also attract like-minded vibrant, happy and positive people and experiences into our lives

CHOOSE SUCCESS

It is all a matter of choice. It really is! We may tell ourselves we'd like to do something, go somewhere, be somebody, but that this, that or the other got in the way and stopped us. Honestly, is that the case? 'I went to the wrong school, didn't have the right education, didn't have forward-thinking parents, wasn't talented enough at an early age; I'm too old now, too busy, I have the children, my wife, parents, friends to think of.' Does anything sound familiar? I would guess that at some point most of us have used one or more of the excuses listed above. 'Excuses?' I hear you cry. Excuses, yes, because that's what they are.

As your coach there is one basic rule about how we're going to work together: we will be honest with each other at all times. I will not mince my words. I will tell you exactly what I think, and consequently you must be true to yourself. What you get from this commitment of absolute honesty is a conviction that we will be able to do the work that needs to be done.

Get Motivated – 7 Steps to the Life You Want is designed for you to cut to the chase. You can spend years worrying about and contemplating life and what you really want. But until you take action all your dreams and ambitions will remain just that: dreams and ambitions. I want you to step forward, challenge yourself to begin doing something. Decide now that you want to progress. If you know what you want, great; if not, that's okay. I often talk to people who know they want to progress, but don't quite know how. The truth is we spend most of our lives panicking about tomorrow, when we should be looking at what needs to be done today.

What you will get from taking action is first and foremost a boost to your energy and motivation. I don't believe this will be your first step, because you've been taking them your whole life. Be thankful for the experience; it is going to be your power, your foundation force for moving forward. So, step up and dream *big*. Relax and enjoy the journey, for together we will make your wonderful, magical, *perfect* life become reality!

> *You will either step forward into growth or you will step back into safety*
>
> **ABRAHAM MASLOW**

DES'S STORY

I worked with Des two years ago. He was alone, separated from his wife, and quite at a loss as to what to do next. A successful property developer for some fifteen years, he worked hard, his life full of people. A trait I noticed immediately was that Des lived on his mobile – he just wouldn't turn it off.

He had intended to be coached on relationship issues, but the constant telephone interruptions disrupted both the general session and Des's train of thought. I asked Des to brainstorm his current beliefs regarding work and time management, which, while highlighting the telephone situation, very quickly brought us right back to relationships and how they had been suffering under his 24/7 attitude to business. For Des it was a real eye-opener.

The main underlying belief we found was that he needed to be the best at everything, at all costs. For Des, this translated into business. Everything and everybody came second, even his own wellbeing. Relationships? They would just have to take a back seat.

Married and divorced three times, commitment had been forthcoming, but only after business had been attended to. I asked Des if his list of priorities was in the right order, or needed to be re-evaluated.

After three sessions, during which he concentrated hard, but still answered calls every couple of minutes,

I called a halt to our coaching. I told him that I admired his focus, but for forty minutes per week we needed his complete, undivided attention. If he was serious about coaching, then he would give me that commitment.

I am telling you this particular part of Des's story to demonstrate one area of beliefs: that of motivation. Until it is an absolute must, and not just a should, could, maybe, or whatever, then it won't get done. If we believe we positively must change in whatever area we're addressing, then change is indeed possible.

I must say, it was with great humility that, three months later, Des called me again and accepted that now he really needed coaching; he wanted his family back, so no more calls.

From that day on coaching with Des was a joy. He was focused, hardworking and so much fun to work with. He not only improved his way of doing business (working smarter instead of just harder), but also renewed his, still ongoing, relationship with his wife. In short, Des turned his life around. In the process, he had to look at and challenge some of his deepest, darkest fears: namely his beliefs. One such fear for Des was that he hadn't seen his dream, his core, in years, and what scared him most was that this central dynamo might no longer be there.

FIND YOUR CORE, FACE YOUR FEAR

Are you strong enough to take a look? Believe me, for most it's a doddle. A real eye-opener, very empowering, a great experience. Sometimes we meet a real bad apple, a gremlin of a belief, as I call it, that needs picking up and moving out (and we will deal with them later in the book), though with focus and resolve this, too, can be easy

Ask yourself what made you have that reaction, whatever it was: for instance, to lose your temper, to burst out laughing with joy. Why did I hate cabbage until my mid-thirties? Was it because I was always forced to eat it as a child, or because my mother never forced me to eat it? My belief that cabbage would taste foul lasted well into my adult years, until one day I questioned it, challenged it head-on – by eating it – and realised the great taste and goodness I'd been missing out on all those years!

This is typical of how not understanding our beliefs, or keeping the wrong ones can hold us back, and also how such action can impact our lives in such a myriad of ways. Because I was always known for being 'picky' with food and for not liking vegetables (and I was never forced), so the persona grew until in my thirties my diet became so unhealthy that at one point I decided I must look for a better option. Within a very short time I added so much nutrition and taste to what had become an extremely bland, processed diet, that I began really to appreciate and enjoy my food in a way I had never done before, with the added bonus of feeling much fitter and healthier.

THE WORK

1. Buy yourself a 'positivity journal'. This will be your workbook, your point of reference, and your fountain of knowledge and inspiration. The only rule about how you use it is that only *positive* ideas and actions can be written down.

2. What would you do if you knew you couldn't fail? Close your eyes and turn the clock forward six months. Imagine your new, future self: achieving all you want, being successful, shining in every way. Spend at least fifteen minutes focusing on this vision. Make it as real as possible. Add sound, colour, smell, taste, feeling.

3. Your ideal life. As soon as you open your eyes, write at least a page describing your ideal life in six months. Again, add and embellish – the more 'real' you make your dream, the more powerful it will become, and the more certain it will become a reality.

4. Now, ask yourself the following questions and write down the answers.

- Who am I when I'm feeling really happy?
- Who am I when I'm feeling really sad?
- How do I see me?
- How do others see me?
- Are there any differences between the two?

5. Where's the proof? Spend the next week looking for evidence that what you want is possible. Cut out similar success stories from newspapers and magazines to stick in your positivity journal. Read a biography of a favourite character's success story. See that it is in fact possible. Notice the operative word there: fact. Support your dream, your vision with fact. *It is possible.*

Key idea

We can't know the answer without asking the question, so be brave enough to ask yourself: 'What do I really want out of this life?'

2

Creating Your Action Plan

Choose a job you love, and you will never work a day in your life

CONFUCIUS

In this chapter I want you to become clear about where you're going, and why. By knowing and documenting your intent, when the going gets tough your dream won't vanish – you'll stand your ground. You will stay on course, or even if you get blown off you'll have enough reason to get back on. One comment I hear constantly when I'm coaching is this: 'I know I feel focused and revved up now, but what happens after a few days?' I'll tell you what happens after a few days: you rely on a good, supportive, well-thought-out plan of action. Without it, even the best of intentions may flounder. With it, you have a chance to stay the course.

One of the first things I do when I start coaching a new client is ask them whether they have an action plan. If they don't, which to be honest is the case with most, we develop one, though even with the few who do we examine if theirs is the right one for them. A good plan should contain not only a step-by-step course to getting where you want to go, but should also remind you why you're going there in the first place. One of the main reasons for failure is that we forget that fundamental justification and consequently lose our way.

Having a plan of action, a commitment to a set of predetermined and measured goals that will keep us on course to achieve our dream, is paramount. An action plan is the reason we have electricity at all times, why television entertains us each evening, and why the local bakery has freshly baked bread to sell us each morning. Imagine your reaction to power cuts because the provider forgot to schedule enough staff to work, or turning on the television to find your favourite programme has simply been forgotten about, or the bakery didn't order any flour this week. Outrage, I would imagine! The truth is that we all use action plans, schedules: they provide almost everything we need to live and enjoy life in a modern society.

What's your reason for wanting to make life better? Why do you want to get there? Justify the success you want by asking yourself the following questions:

- What will achieving this add to my life?
- Will it make me happier?
- Will it make me healthier?
- Will it make me more prosperous?
- Will it improve my relationships with other people?
- What might I lose from my current life by achieving this?
- Will I miss what has gone?
- Will I regret leaving it behind?

And finally:

- What is my justification for achieving this new part of my life?

Spend some time on the final point, and add the answer to your positivity journal. Remember, keep the tone positive, light; this is something you'll be so excited about you just can't help but go for it.

A plan of action, supported by reasons why it will work, is an absolute prerequisite for any success strategy, which is what we are building. I want you to carry on the feeling of focus long after you've put this book down and keep the momentum going, increase it and achieve far in excess of what you ever thought possible.

It's amazing how many of us don't have any plan. Imagine buying a ticket on a train, an open ticket to anywhere. You have no idea where you want to go or how much time you'd like to spend travelling before you get there. How will you know when you've arrived? Where exactly is 'there'? What if your destination is exactly the place you wouldn't have chosen to be? After all, you had no plan, so how could you complain?

I want to convince you that it is possible to achieve your desires. And the way to do it is to focus on where you ultimately want to go in life. It's not so much your goals but the grand design you should be considering right now; just how far will you let your imagination take you? I'm talking about the big picture. What's yours? Identifying what you really want and having the courage to go for it is the basis of all self-development. If we strive for something less than our true desire, or aim to achieve solely because we imagine it's what is expected of us, many of us will fail. Unless our values and beliefs inform the choices we make and the plans we create, all our efforts will be wasted.

BE ONE OF THE TOP 3 PER CENT!

It's vital that you write things down. Every exercise, every plan, every goal should be recorded and, most importantly, reread frequently. Your positivity journal should be something special: it will, after all, carry your life plan. 'But why the need to write everything down?' I hear you ask. Because the more of our senses we use, the greater impact the work will have.

The need for well-thought-out, written-down goals and motivation is well documented. In 1947 the top hundred students at Yale University were asked about their life and career plans. Twenty years later, researchers revisited the hundred ex-students and what they found was startling:

Bring in' a T.V photo copy a page — use it

- Only 3 per cent had actually written down the life goals and plans they had spoken about.
- But, significantly, that 3 per cent had achieved success and amassed wealth greater than the other 97 per cent put together! *to begin' the discussion!*

Of course, the research covered much more than just the creation of wealth, but for the sake of this exercise it highlights in a very quantifiable way the importance of written-down, formulated planning. A pragmatic, goal-oriented approach to life, and the coaching process that results from it are essential. In short, we need a plan.

GET A DIARY

Have a what's on in my life.

Or better still, use the one cousin George bought you last Christmas! Do you use a daily planner? If not, why not? If you think your life is not busy enough, then why do you buy a television guide, a 'what's on' movie guide, or follow a recipe so that you don't burn that new dish you want to try, or find out the time of the

we plan what we went to
watch on the

T.v if we put so much effort into 1 day or a week what could next bus or train? By doing any or all of these things, what you're saying is that it's okay for you to follow these other plans and schedules, but your life isn't important enough to do the same for what really matters to you: your future.

If you were to plan a whole week, what kind of things would be included? For the purposes of this exercise, write down each day on a piece of A4 paper, and then brainstorm. American peak performance coach Anthony Robbins refers to 'the six human needs': certainty, uncertainty, significance, contribution, personal growth and love. For our life to be in balance, we, at some level, need constantly to address and attempt to meet all six of these fundamental needs. Look back over your weekly 'brainstorm' schedule, and see what areas of life you're addressing. If everything relates only to work (which is common), try adding tasks that deal with other areas.

Have a look at the following specimen list, and see if you can decide which areas of human need are being addressed:

- Must call five business contacts
- Do workout at the gym
- Spend one hour reading a book
- Call mum and sister
- Have coffee with a friend
- Enrol in new evening class

Does that list cover all the human needs, or does it lack some important areas? Now take another look at yours, and ask, 'How can I make it even more representative of who I truly am as a person, and who I want to become?'

Successful self-development needs to be regular and constant, something always at the forefront of our minds; we need to read about, write about, and imagine our success constantly. This in itself will make what we do much more potent. If we think about our perfect life enough it will eventually happen. After all, repetition is the mother of all success, isn't it?

Nancy Ashley wrote in her ground-breaking book, *Create Your Own Reality*, that we do indeed have absolute control over what we achieve in our lives, the good and the bad. Therefore it is our obligation to move forward and heighten our lives. We can blame no one or any event for holding us back. Taking on complete responsibility in this way will motivate us to make the most of our life.

TAKE CHARGE OF YOUR LIFE

I told you I know how exciting but daunting it was to make those first steps towards transforming your life into the one of your dreams. I still remember buying my first motivational book more than sixteen years ago. It was *Take Charge of Your Life* by Luis Proto.

Amazing stuff. At the time I was a small-town boy living in Grantham, Lincolnshire. Not a bad little town, and of course for many years now I've enjoyed going back regularly to visit family and friends. But as a young man in the early and mid-eighties Grantham felt like a prison.

I had always been a shy boy, and suffered a severe stammer for most of my early life. Indeed, until the age of twenty-four or so just saying my name was a near impossibility. School and college teachers would avoid asking me questions in class – which I now understand was as much to avoid their own embarrassment as mine.

Solace came in the shape of my music teacher, Mr Winter, a man I have not seen in more than two decades, but to whom I owe so much, not least my early sanity. An organist at the local church, he was a great storyteller of his many adventures touring throughout Europe during long summer holidays. Here was someone who rose above my impediment, and ultimately introduced me to both singing and the trombone. Suddenly, I could communicate without fear of laughter and ridicule, and for the first time in my life I experienced the joy of standing on stage, an audience of all ages listening to me with undivided attention, and even applauding. To this day, I do not know of a more liberating sensation. Even now, the delight of being able to open my mouth and hear a stream of coherent, unhalting words makes me feel both humble and grateful. Those early, harsh years gave me the motivation to live the life I lead today.

My stammer lessened during my twenties. I had read an article in a magazine explaining how hypnotherapy might help, and I made an appointment straight away. Even then I knew I would only solve this problem through my own efforts. Once you decide to take charge of your life, assuming total responsibility for your success and failure, that fundamental knowledge cannot be unlearned. For me it was quite simply earth-shattering, a real ground-breaking moment – and I loved it. No one could stop me now unless I wanted or allowed them to. Luis Proto's book, for me, began a chain reaction that still changes my life to this day.

Many years ago an old friend gave me a piece of advice, wisdom I could not quite grasp at the time, but for which I have since been grateful many times over: 'There is only one thing more frightening than moving forward and that is standing still.' Think about it. We are frozen with fear so many times at the prospect of taking a chance, of seizing the opportunity, of jumping into the unknown. But standing still, staying where we are, repeating possibly for ever the frustration of what has become our present – surely that is much worse? If we are lucky we will learn this lesson quickly, though all too often it takes the better part of a lifetime. How many times have you heard an older person comment,

'Oh, I wish I'd taken that chance. If I had my time over again I'd . . .'

If I can achieve one thing with this book, it is to make you take that first step; create your own reality – don't just exist in whatever happens to be around you and 'go with the flow'. How awful. How boring a life that would be. Make your own flow. Make your world something special, something simply amazing!

Your dream is your potential reality. What you focus on will manifest itself. What you believe you will become. Believe 'it' (whatever 'it' is) will happen, and guess what? Your best life becomes possible. This book is about opening up that dream, stepping forward with a rock-solid plan of action that enables you to achieve a better life. But to begin I need you to have an open mind and truly believe that at some point soon your unique, fabulous dream will develop into reality before your very eyes.

CAROLINE'S STORY

I started working with one young lady, Caroline, last year. I remember her first telephone call, in which she described herself as 'wanting to be a professional singer'. What this meant in practice was that Caroline was a semi-professional singer: she sang part time. Fine. But there are two types of semi-professional singer: the one who only wants to pursue music as a pastime, who figures that if it supplements their weekly income that's a bonus, but that it's essentially an enjoyable hobby. And then there's the other kind, like Caroline, who always wanted something altogether more serious: she wanted a career.

At first, Caroline came across as very focused and serious about her art. I asked how she was going to 'make it' in the world of showbiz, and I got a very enthusiastic, powerful answer; Caroline was very passionate. But when we came down to specifics – what she was actually going to do this month, next quarter, by the end of the year – solid, quantifiable goals suddenly dissipated and energy blew away. I was left facing a girl who desperately wanted to become a singer because, well, just because she wanted to.

I explained the importance of mapping out an action plan and supporting it with reasons why specific targets had to be achieved, the stronger the reasons the better. Even though at first Caroline was nervous of getting passionate about why she wanted success so much, with not too much encouragement the whole story came tumbling out. So often we are not used to justifying why we want something. As children we are completely vocal with our mothers – 'I want, I want, I want . . . because . . .' – but by adulthood we somehow become more reserved, or, I would say, shy, even lazy, in the justification stakes. If I could give one important piece of advice here, it's to get more vocal, both with yourself and other people. Tell the world what you want and you just might get it; don't say anything, and how are we all supposed to be psychic?

Caroline wanted to achieve a better life, a life of dreams and travel and premières, concerts, entertaining and helping people, and becoming very wealthy indeed. Phew! Now she had reasons for being a singer. Remember, the more vivid we make our dreams, the harder we work to translate them into reality.

Next came the plan of action, which is a 'work in progress', since once it is developed it can always be amended, improved, tweaked and used to record successes and milestones. Breakthroughs can also be noted in the positivity journal.

Over the next few weeks we worked on Caroline's action plan. What began as an aspiration supported by nothing concrete became something solid and focused. In short, Caroline moved from someone who 'wanted to be a singer' to a professional artist working in recording studios, tours, theatre and most recently television.

YOUR STORY!

What's your story? What has brought you to the place you're at in life right now? Do you know what's good and what's not? What about the journey you've made so far? What's worked and what hasn't? Simply by being aware of the highs and lows, and then making a conscious decision to learn positively from as much as you can will, with one stroke, alter your focus. Imagine, from this moment on, always to be able to learn something positive from any and every situation. No more regrets, no more 'what ifs' and definitely no more sweeping embarrassing episodes under that carpet in your mind! This is an exercise for your positivity journal. Knowing who you are and why you're planning to do what you say you want to do is invaluable.

Using that same journal, increasingly full of the best of who you are, is also a great point of reference during times of doubt or uncertainty to remind you why you're doing this, what your objectives are and the huge potential offered by living life at its best!

use this well in my ner bodiler

QUESTIONS TO ASK *yourself*.

- Why am I doing this?
- What is/are my goal(s), my ultimate point of arrival?
- What can I do to support myself along the way?
- If the going gets tough, how can I continue?
- How can I ensure that I follow through on actions I schedule?
- How can I reward myself, and when should I reward myself for doing this work?

THE WORK

1. The Wheel of Life

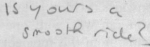

Is yours a smooth ride?

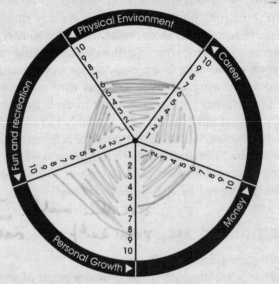

Draw your Wheel of Life in your journal using the diagram above as a guide. Fill in each segment as indicated with an important area of your life. I've given some general examples, but as we are all unique you should enter areas that are most relevant to you. Rate your level of satisfaction with each area, out of ten. Ten would indicate you're successful, fabulous in every way. Five would suggest average (and who wants to be that?) One? Let's just say we have some work to do! Then draw a line from point to point to connect the spokes. If the wheel is smooth and round you will have a pleasant ride and go a long way. But if each area of the wheel is uneven and jagged, no matter what you do, life won't be so easy. How bumpy would the ride be if this were a real wheel?

2. Imagine your success. For each area not yet a ten, identify one way in which you would know if it were. 'I'd feel fantastic,' isn't enough; it has to be something quantifiable. For example, if I wanted to improve the fun and recreation area I might pinpoint dancing with friends at least twice a month and joining a weekly salsa class as markers of success. These markers should be something concrete you could revisit in six months to assess your progress.

3. Set your goals. Once you've identified your dreams, you can decide on the first steps needed to achieve them. If you only scored six in an area, you need to improve the rating by four points. So, what would your first four tasks be? Examine each area in turn similarly.

4. Schedule success. When will you do the work? Do you have time tomorrow, next Wednesday, or aren't you sure when you'll be able to fit it in? This is the wrong attitude. Decide when you will work at a task and then commit to it. Use your diary. If someone calls up for a chat or to meet for coffee when you have a task scheduled explain that you will be busy. Tell them if you want, but don't change your mind. Of course, if something really important comes along, be flexible, but generally once you commit to a goal, stick to it.

5. Get moving! There really is no substitute for taking action. The bigger the action, the tougher the goal is to achieve, the better. Imagine you have a list of thirty things to do this week, and you have six scheduled for today; put the most difficult, the ones you would really rather avoid at the top and do them first. The payback for this course of action will be immense. You'll feel a million dollars, which you'll be able to feed off tomorrow when you have your next clutch of goals to achieve.

Key idea

Our bodies are what we eat, our mind is what we think, and our heart is what we dream – so dream big and plan hard.

use this quote on wheel –

3

The Proactive Approach

The secret of success in life is to be ready for opportunity when it comes

BENJAMIN DISRAELI

That quote is one of my favourites ever. The simplicity belies its absolute message: be ready and waiting for opportunity, so that when it comes you just go for it. Or, as Henry T. Ford so eloquently put it, 'Whether you think you can or you think you can't, you're probably right.'

By the end of this chapter I want you to be chomping at the bit, ready to take action. One piece of advice I want to give here is this: don't wait until you've read the whole book before you get going. Why on earth would you want to wait? Believe me, there isn't a breakthrough, a final insight waiting for you on the last page. I hope that you'll find loads of ideas to inspire how to put this fabulous new life together along the way. I'm not saving myself for the last page, and I don't want you to do that either.

'But life is so busy; there are so many differing, conflicting demands that don't even touch my needs, my dreams, where I want to go.' I hear you, believe me, I do. Trying to juggle a thousand and one things, and fulfil all those life dreams can seem impossible. I couldn't agree with you more, which is why we have a little 'must' rule coming into the equation here: you must prioritise.

PRIORITISE TO SUCCEED

Prioritise to succeed instead of slamming into everything like a bull in a china shop. Not very empowering. I know some people have a problem with lists; they always sounded so dreary to me. As a child and teenager I used to look at women pushing a trolley around Sainsbury's clinging desperately to their shopping lists, or at besuited businessmen ticking off their lists of 'things to do' while leaning on their briefcase on the bus or tube. Not cool, I thought. Of course, now I realise my attitude was just that, a severe case of teenage angst.

Nowadays I happily make my lists, fill in my schedules and allocate time to my heart's content. I'm in control; and if on occasion I see a bullish gaze come my way from a teenager I smile right back and think, You're going to wake up and do this one day as well, I hope, because then you'll know that you're not going to waste even a minute of this wonderful, precious time we're all given.

Priorities are so important. In the last exercise we introduced the concept of the Wheel of Life: the idea that your life is made up of several, quite distinct, important areas. It's easy to get caught up in one thing sometimes, but ignoring others doesn't mean they simply go away; rather the longer we leave them out in the cold the more attention they might need in the future to put right again. Self-awareness in this area is really all about self-maintenance and knowing what your priorities are is essential for a sustainable life.

525,600 MINUTES   *intro - to wheel exercise*

Or 8,760 hours. One year. It can be as long, or as short, as you want it to be. How do you fill yours? Do you use your time wisely, or waste it, frittering, worrying, 'clock-watching' your life away? It's not that I'm suggesting every moment has to be scheduled and allocated a job; life should be more spontaneous than that. But, equally, your time is precious – some would say it's your most valuable asset – and should be valued accordingly.

do this big & in different size text

BACK TO THE FUTURE

Imagine for a moment you're a very old version of who you are today. Maybe you're seventy, eighty or ninety – it's different for everyone. The idea is you're still healthy, probably grey, and very mature. You're sitting with a young person, maybe a child or teenager, a relative. This person is very interested in what you have to say, and you love talking to this person. They ask you to tell them stories from your long life, about how it used to be, what you did, how you coped. What would you tell them? What would the high points have been? Where did you live? Were you married, or single, in a relationship? Did you have children? What ambitions did you achieve? This, of course, is the positive version. Maybe the questions you'll imagine are more about what you missed, how you sold yourself short, or when you simply were not brave enough to step up and take action. If this is the case, what did you miss as a result? What did it cost you in terms of self-esteem, confidence, love and, yes, money?

Coming back to the present, what did you learn from this future insight? We don't realise it, but the point at which most of us give up is just one step away from success. Which do you think is the hardest lift to make at the gym, or the most difficult lap to run at the track: the first or the last? It is the last, of course. So tell me, which has the most influence, will create the strongest muscle, or the greatest stamina? The last, of course, always the last.

TIME

By prioritising, you should be able to free up time to get your life moving in a higher, more effective gear. But what would you do with that time? And where exactly could you find even more of it?

- Many of my clients now listen to their language/ motivational/study CDs while driving to and from work each day; they switched the myriad music channels off and now feel so much more empowered because of it
- Other people cut down from a daily (over) dose of anything up to seven or eight soap operas. It's tough in the beginning, but believe me cutting down will give you a whole new life – typically between seven and ten hours per week (and that's not even including the three-hour 'omnibuses' on a Sunday)
- Mums who previously felt completely excluded from 'self-help' possibilities now thrive just because they worked out a baby/child sitting schedule with grand-parents/aunts/uncles/best friends with offspring – and notice I haven't even mentioned paid-for child-care yet. How many after-school/school holiday activities can a child get before they overdose?

Answer: it's infinite! We're talking 'win-win' here

The watchword is to try all possibilities. What's the worst that could happen if it didn't work out? You have to try again, reconsider, come up with another angle, but with the same outcome in mind: fitting extra personal development time into your life.

WORK/LIFE BALANCE

Prioritising is rarely easy, especially when it comes to the important things. Tom is a jobbing actor, he travels a lot and has a very busy schedule.

Tom suffers the age-old dilemma, in that he's worked for years as a struggling actor, doing every 'day job' under the sun (builder, barman, waiter, admin., the list goes on), yet now when his career is finally coming together life somehow isn't feeling 'right' any more.

When we looked a little deeper, other areas of Tom's life came into focus. He is in a long-term relationship, and they have a young daughter. Tom made a decision last year to 'go for it' career-wise; and now as work is flooding in, he feels he doesn't see his daughter or girl-friend anything like as much as he wants.

We all juggle many different areas of our lives. Mostly, somewhere in the equation we have home life and work to contend with. Of course, there's loads of other stuff going on: friends, health and fitness, money, family and, hopefully, personal development (to name but a few). That's the point: we do have to juggle it all, otherwise sooner rather than later things will start to feel missed out, things will stop happening in a way that 'feels right'. In short, we'll begin to feel more than a little frayed at the edges.

Work/life balance in an ideal, *relaxed*, carefree world would just happen naturally. But when our life gets too busy, or we've slackened off and let everything drift a little, we need to reassess our work/life balance. In the real world, it doesn't just 'happen', it has to be worked on.

Every one of us has demands coming from all directions, but we can always choose what kind of response we make to those demands. We have the opportunity to do the best we can for ourselves.

Remember: coaching is about moving forward from where you are now to where you want to be. It is for the walking well. We can all use a coach sometimes!

SELF-MANAGEMENT

Are you a good manager – of yourself? What qualities do you think a good manager should have? And what should they not have? Take a look at the following list and tick off the attributes that you would identify with, and then add others that are missing – those more personal to you.

What makes a great manager?

- Flexibility
- Strength
- Leadership
- Direction
- Resolve
- Focus
- Knowledge
- Listening
- Support

What doesn't make a great manager?

- Small-mindedness
- Closed attitude

STAY FOCUSED

Naomi Watts is an enigma, known for so many years as the best friend of Nicole Kidman. Always the one asked to stand aside when photographs were being taken, the 'who's your friend?' kind of lady. Naomi was always focused, she always knew where she wanted to go, and even though Hollywood took a while to recognise her talent, it didn't mean she believed herself to be any the less actress or person.

After more than ten years doing bit parts in movies and on television it was in Alejandro Gonzalez Inarritu's Oscar-winning *21 Grams* that the world was finally introduced to Naomi Watts's undoubted talent. Now suddenly a whole host of other projects are lined up for her, directors want to direct her, fellow actors want to work with her, and the audience want to see her develop and grow in her craft.

This Kent-born, Welsh- and Australian-raised actress is a shining example of how staying focused and prioritising keeps you on track to win through. It was by remaining in Hollywood, taking the jobbing roles, and appearing in the David Lynch movie *Mulholland Drive* that finally the breakthrough came. Now, of course, she's lined up to star opposite actors such as Ewan McGregor and Sean Penn in movies such as *Stay*, *The Assassination of Richard Nixon*, even *King Kong*!

You will already have ideas on several different levels of what you want to do. You may have a dream, a reason why you bought this book, which will be unique to you. Your partner, children, career, finances, health – there are always many things vying for position, a chunk of your time. But since no matter what we do there will only ever be twenty-four hours in each day, we have to make choices about what to concentrate on and what not along the way.

CARRIE'S STORY

'What do you really want?' is a question I ask all clients, usually more than once, and when they feel relaxed enough with me the floodgates to their dreams and ambitions open. It's quite noticeable that we can go from clipped, polite conversation and well-thought-out answers to flowing, rushing tirades of inspiration – and so it was with Carrie.

What began as a strained 'I don't really know' became a long list of ideas, plans, goals, dreams to achieve, places to go, people to meet: Carrie became a real inspiration.

The only problem was that Carrie's dreams went into orbit! I always encourage people to dream, and dream big. In the words of Marianne Williamson: 'Who are you to play small?' I don't ask you to think practically, at least not at the beginning. At some point, however, you will filter out the pipe dreams. Then, if you really want to do something, just go ahead and do it. If in the doing you realise it's not what you wanted after all then fine, at least you tried; you gave it your best shot. Now you can move on and do something else. So many people never even get to that point. I don't want you to become one of them.

Carrie dreamed big, yet played small. She would talk about the most inspirational, powerful life, committing to long lists of action, planning 'things to do',

yet the following week we'd ⌐
on why she hadn't achieved he⌐
commit yourself 100 per cent, b⌐
because then you risk being overwh⌐
ing 25 per cent or less. That's not emp⌐
a thin line between total commitm⌐
commitment. How will you know? You⌐
the difference between feeling challenged
panic. Trial and error, and being able to ⌐ ⌐sess
constantly is essential.

Consider the postage stamp: its usefulness consists in
the ability to stick to one thing till it gets there

JOSH BILLINGS

GETTING STARTED

So, what can you do today that will make a difference? Something you haven't done before, that isn't
a 'soft option', which will stretch you a little and make
you feel a million dollars for having achieved it? Would
it be to make that difficult call, talk to your manager,
or join the acting group? What is it? You know. Every
one of us knows not only what we should be doing,
but also how to get there. There will be easier, smaller
steps of course, but which ones will give you the

...especially at the beginning? Right: the

...remember a few years ago when I worked in banking and felt very disgruntled with my lot. Everything was wrong, and I thought it all needed changing. My hours were too long, I was underpaid, over-pressured, undervalued – you get the idea. Every day I felt like marching in to my manager, Mark's office and telling him a few home truths. My world was not a happy one. Thankfully for me, though, Mark was a pretty enlightened fellow. He'd studied more than a little NLP (Neuro Linguistic Programming, which is essentially the science of creating rapport and connecting). We'd had lots of conversations comparing the many self-help books we'd read over the years; I'd worked alongside him for the best part of a year; and even though we had all this in common I still forgot the art of communication at that point, due entirely, I now know, to the stress levels I was placing on myself.

'So, what's up, Mike?' he said. 'You've got a face like a wet weekend. Spill.' And he sat there until I did. We talked. I didn't scream and shout, but I didn't shrink away from what I needed to say either. For his part, Mark just listened. Ordinarily, he was a great talker himself, but on that day I did the talking. If he started to say something, I would, with respect, ask him to let me continue; I needed to say my piece.

The result? Just to talk had relieved some of the

immediate pressure. But also my workload was reduced, my hours brought back to some sort of normality, and a long overdue pay rise implemented. But what had really happened? I'll tell you: I had taken back responsibility, and in doing so had upgraded the value I had in myself tenfold. I had control over my life again.

The payoff for not taking positive action is relinquishing our personal power. That hurts. It lowers the regard we have for ourselves. Yet by setting a course of action and following through with it one step at a time, and most importantly not shying away from the tougher tasks, you raise your self-esteem by a mile.

BECOME PROACTIVE

To conclude, the all-important first decision you must make is to be proactive. No matter how wonderful your dream, or how detailed and expertly laid out your plan is, without taking consistent action nothing will ever come of it. Second, with such a busy and demanding life, prioritising is an absolute must. Without taking the time to decide where to begin, and where exactly to focus your energies, they will dissipate. A scattergun approach doesn't work; at best you will become frustrated, at worst, disillusioned. Third, make a start! That's it: begin today. Don't plan to start when you're all prepared, next week, or (even worse) next month. Begin this very moment. No matter how small, or how big your first action is, do it – and do it with all the heart and passion you can muster. Above all, taking action will send a message to your brain that 'Yes, I mean business.' Nothing builds motivation quicker.

What will those choices be for you? Begin now to understand what your life should be, and what you must do in order to get it.

THE WORK

1. Things to do. What must you do first, second, third this week? I sit down on a Sunday evening and make a 'things to achieve' list for the following week. Number one is to write the list, and don't skimp or try to squeeze it into a couple of minutes; this is your life here, so take time with it. Write down everything that comes to mind, all the little jobs as well as the bigger ones; and don't forget to add fun to the equation – swimming, partying, calling friends (always very important).

2. Get daily. Now, what jumps out and says, 'I should be done on Wednesday', or whatever? Go through each day and allocate tasks to each day (remember, this is still in the planning stage, so all can be changed). Now take the tasks that fall into the 'tougher than the rest' category: you know, the ones that more often than not will still be waiting all on their lonesome ownsome at the end of the week, unaccomplished. Allocate those days, too.

3. The practicality of time. Be practical with your time. This can also be read as 'don't waste your precious time', and 'stick to your agenda' – after all, it is one of your own choosing! So, what time do you have to do this task, take that class, or achieve each and every goal you've set yourself for the week? By this point you should be looking at morning, afternoon, evening, weekday and weekend slots.

4. 28 hours a day. Short of time to fit everything in? Hmm. Do you watch one of the many soaps on TV? What about spending three hours each day commuting? Become aware of the potential extra time you could claw back just by (1), becoming aware of it, and (2), making the required adjustments to free it up.

5. Celebrate success. Seems a little obvious, but tick tasks completed off your schedule as and when you've achieved them. It tells the brain we've done well, which leads to a feeling of satisfaction. Equally, using this method enables us to transfer uncompleted tasks to another day, or even to the next week. But if this happens, those tasks automatically go to the top of the list and *must* be completed before anything else.

Key idea

Don't just plan to live your life tomorrow, decide to live it today.

4

Accessing the Soul

*This above all: to thine own self be true, And it must
follow, as the night the day, Thou canst not then be
false to any man*

WILLIAM SHAKESPEARE

Are you working with the real you in mind? Does
this desire for a better life come from the heart? Do
you aspire to create the life you were born to live? Or
is it because you want what someone else has or enjoys?
Do you dream of being as famous as Brad Pitt, as gifted
as Vanessa Mae, or as successful as George Soros, the
American billionaire investor? All of which are fine and
good, so long as this is what you really want, what your
soul is telling you is your 'life's work'. Knowing what
this truly is, being able to tap into this set of basic beliefs
and instincts is essential if we want to live a fruitful
and focused life, a life of fewer dead-ends.

But what is the soul? Chico Xavier, the Brazilian writer and spiritualist describes it as, 'that which is more than what we are'. It is the core, something that is deeper than our conscious, even our subconscious mind. Nonetheless, it is not separate, but an integral part of who we are.

I believe it is simply our being; what we really are. If this is the case, though, does this mean that in some way, without doing a lot of work, we are not our 'true selves'? 'But I'm honest, a real person,' I hear you protest – and I believe you. In his book *Change Your Life in 7 Days*, Paul McKenna describes how we build up layers to our personality as the years go by. Unintentionally, we become who we need to be in any given situation and with all the many people with whom we come into contact. So we are being real, or at least true to ourselves in that we are who we feel we need to be in life. If, however, you have been living a lie or accommodating others to the exclusion of yourself, then to 'act as if', as a new, more positive person, is a good way to re-educate our habits in order to get to where we want to go. And, if that's you, then reading this book will get you off to a good start.

A good place to begin is your childhood. Think back and try to remember what it was you always wanted to do. Did you want to be a fireman, or a nurse, a scientist, a rock star, or simply the character of your favourite book (how many children today want to become Harry Potter)? Cast your mind back and see again what you saw then, feel what you felt, and be the child you once were. The reason for this is to begin to reconnect with who we really are, by first remembering, and *honouring*, who we once were.

As a child what prompted this dream? How did the prospect make you feel? What was your world like back then? Can you remember your old house, how it felt for you in the smaller sized body you once had? Did you dream your dreams in the garden, or in the house? Was the weather hot, like summertime, or cold and frosty, like winter?

Then consider how those dreams have changed through the years. Are they still the same? Or did they change? If so, did they develop, or are they completely different? Where is the connection between who you are now and who you were then? My connection with my childhood is my desire to communicate – and to help others who are challenged in this area. Through the years it has manifested itself in singing, acting, coaching, writing, and I'm sure many other ways, but the point is that there is a connection, a strand running through my life.

So, what is it for you? You know what you want to do by now, and we have the beginnings of a plan of action. Now look at your reasons for wanting this new achievement in your life.

Becoming more motivated makes life easier, with less

hassle and more possibilities. Conversely, not knowing why you want that better life can lead to years of blind alleys. There have been times in my life when I wanted to achieve something for all the right reasons: I wanted to make someone proud of me, I felt passionately about my cause, I felt I was fighting the good fight, or simply my goal would make me tonnes of money. Without exception, throughout all these times the course was tough, an uphill battle the whole way. I can think of specific examples: wanting to look powerful and successful in front of friends (which is an intoxicating reason in itself) by trying to become this super-successful corporate animal in a power suit with loads of attitude; or turning my hand to stand-up comedy (a very different course indeed, granted). The thread running through both, and several other ventures, was the false belief that if I was successful I would gain approval from others, and so could ultimately 'approve' of myself. Needless to say, my life was hard and not a lot of fun, and I didn't acheive anything like the wealth or success I craved.

Other activities, such as singing, coaching and writing, are things I would do anyway, successful or not; they are just as much part of who I am as the colour of my hair or my height.

How does this idea of doing things and pursuing dreams for the 'right reasons' fit with your goal, whatever it was that initially prompted you to pick up this book? Are we still at the same point? If things have

shifted a little, that's fine, ev~~
one of the lucky ones still o~~
good for you. Believe me: I chan~~
a few times along the way.

FIRING UP YOUR IMAGINATION

Ask yourself the following questions:

- What really gets my imagination going?
- What does my ideal life look like, the one that will result from taking action and from doing the work listed in this book?

Write down your responses. Did you write a lot or a little? Was your dream exciting? Could you visualise the new, future you? Or did you find it difficult? If not, great; now keep writing, keep visualising and carry on reading.

If you struggled, ask yourself if what you're looking for is really you? If it really is, ask yourself:

- Am I playing small, to my true potential?
- Does achieving my ideal life scare me?
- Does the prospect of being truly responsible horrify me?
- What type of person would I have to be in order to go for it?

...ready inside me waiting to get out?
... can I do today that will support this new
...f not, how can I become this new, improved
version of me?

But what if you found this exercise difficult, realising your dreams don't match the real you? Then you really need to look within. Ask yourself:

- Is this my dream, or someone else's?
- Is my dream current, or one I need to let go from the past?
- Would achieving this dream give me the life I truly want?
- If not, what would this 'old' dream actually bring?
- What would this dream *not* bring to my life?

If you knew you couldn't fail, what would the real dream be? Be brave and let your imagination out!

Do you do what you want to in day-to-day life? Or do you find yourself adapting to what you perceive others require of you? In other words, do you do what you feel you 'should', rather than what you truly 'want'? If that's the case, it's for the wrong reason. Sooner or later you'll discover you've hit a brick wall, and it won't feel good. By identifying your true dreams now, you'll save yourself enormous amounts of time. Use the following grid to detail the differences between goals you 'want' to achieve, and those you feel you 'should' be pursuing. What follows is a fair example of what my clients have answered over the years. How true do they ring for you?

A. What Would I Like To Do?	B. What Do I Feel I Should Do?
I would like to travel the world	I feel I should stay in control
I would like to run the London marathon	I feel I should be logical
I would like to spend a large amount of money pampering myself and have bright blonde highlights put in my hair	I feel I should stay in the '9 to 5' treadmill for everyone else's sake
I'd like to sit on a beach in Portugal, totally alone, listening to the waves and being at one with nature	I feel I should work hard
I'd like to 'go wild' and let my hair down at least once a month	I feel I have to conform and seek others' approval

A. What Would I Like To Do? (cont.)	B. What Do I Feel I Should Do? (cont.)
I'd like to be famous	I feel I should be overwhelmed with my lot
I'd like to do the work I really want to do	I feel I should stay 'small', not to upset or threaten anyone
I'd like to be loved for who I am, instead of who others would like me to be	I feel I should be part of the team

1. Be honest. Fill in the following grid according to your own beliefs and experience.

2. Ask yourself the key question. How can I move away from B and live more of my life in A?

3. Look back to your plan of action. Check that your aims and ambitions fit under the heading A.

4. What do you notice is the difference between the two columns? What do you imagine the cost of living such a life would be? Do you think people with these conflicts live a balanced and fruitful life?

A. What Would I Like To Do?	B. What Do I Feel I Should Do?

There is nothing wrong with switching tracks, especially if you realise you're pursuing the wrong dream. At that point, stop and take time out to reassess. That is much more empowering than to continue regardless, aware you're not listening to your true self.

Map it out, write it down, and above all *act on it*. Never, ever do this type of work then file it away in the back of a drawer, only to be rediscovered in a year's time. What a waste that would be.

I want you to discover not only what it is you want and why, but also to make it a permanent force in your life, long after reading this book. Your soul is your secret weapon, your ultimate ally. If you take the time to listen it will never lie or lead you in the wrong direction.

HOW INTUITIVE ARE YOU?

When was the last time you actually listened to your soul? Some call it your heart, intuition, or sixth sense; I call it the truth, for it doesn't know how to lie. We've often read about people surprising themselves by the truth of their hunches. There is the familiar sensation of thinking of a person who then phones us at that moment or appears at the door. And there are the times when we go out of our way to do something new despite all our friends' advice not to, that it won't work. Yet when we've succeeded all we can say is that we *knew* it would work, we could just 'feel' it. Hmm.

On the other hand, I remember reading the story of a man who lost millions in a financial deal, the like of which he'd made his fortune at a hundred times before. But this time felt different for him. Afterwards he said that although he knew what he was doing and felt his experience would carry him through, something he couldn't quite put his finger on just hadn't felt right. Of course, he'd overruled that emotion and told himself not to be so silly – and the rest, as they say, is history.

Some call it an access to the soul; others help from above; while the more pragmatic among us attempt to explain it as a yet unidentified energy awareness similar to some animals' capacity to 'smell' danger or sense an advantageous situation. Whatever it is, it helps us – if we give it the opportunity. It can help you on your way, stop you wasting time on the wrong things, and keep you on course with the good.

But how can you know the difference between moments of inspiration and others when all you hear is the voice of doubt? Ask yourself if what you're proposing will be for the positive or the negative. Even if you're working your way out of a negative situation, asking if your intended actions will be for the greater good will be a starting point.

TONY'S STORY

After several weeks of coaching without making much

headway I confronted Tony with a few blunt questions to find out if he did indeed want to be coached, or not. A family man, Tony was in his mid-forties, had been married to Jane for fourteen years and had three children. Tony owned his own media publishing company, was ultra busy, but equally focused on keeping a good family life.

On the face of it, Tony sounded as though he had an idyllic, successful life, one the rest of us might aspire to. Except that Tony was a lost man. He had been running on automatic for so long, seemingly with great results, that for the most part he had not seen the signs that he was losing control of what he had created.

At first I thought it was simply a case of switching tracks: Tony had told me how he'd grown tired of his business and dreamed of starting again with another concern. He had it all worked out, handing over management, while keeping ownership, and the new start-up strategy. We looked at how all this would affect and fit into his current life: everything was going fine except for one thing. Week after week Tony would come to our sessions with a list of excuses as to why nothing had happened or been achieved since our previous meeting. He would have been too busy, this had happened unexpectedly, that had put a spanner in the works. Excuses.

Finally, I suggested Tony go on a little voyage of discovery, set aside the coaching agenda for a while and engage his soul. I asked him to suspend his judgement and 'become' nineteen again; to explain to his wife that for a few short weeks he might do the unexpected and be unconventional. First, I asked Tony to describe his perfect location – with the intelligence of an adult, but the innocence and playfulness of a teenager. Portugal came up. He had this vision of walking along a deserted beach in late summer, trousers rolled up, barefoot, watching and listening to the gulls skimming the surface of the ocean. I asked if he'd ever taken this holiday; he hadn't. Would he like to? Yes, he would. You can guess what happened next . . .

A week later he called me for our next coaching session – from a little place just south of Lisbon! This time I talked to a very different man. Even the tone of his voice was more relaxed. I had planned to ask Tony to begin a dream accessing exercise, but the floodgates were already open. This time he could just let his dreams and desires roll out from the very centre of his being. These were not PC, in control, mid-life successful businessman dreams; these were the essence of what could so easily make him begin to tick all over again.

Out came all the worry and angst that had been filed away in his subconscious for so many years, all the petty arguments and unresolved 'stuff' from an otherwise successful marriage, even old grudges from his school days. I asked Tony to decide if he still needed or could effect a resolution to these past troubles, or whether it would simply be best to let things go, in a spirit of understanding and relinquishment. And over the next week he carried out the latter course. On a couple of occasions he felt he should write letters (which he wouldn't send) explaining how he had felt, followed by the replies containing what he would have wanted the other parties to say (all of which he would destroy after the exercise). He found the whole process completely liberating.

When we talked a week later he described feeling as though a huge weight had been lifted from his life. Even though none of this had been apparent before, these emotions had been festering for all those years. Now Tony felt they had been understood and removed. He was elated.

We resumed our coaching. But from this point on Tony was a much more self-assured and happier man, because now he felt in tune with who he really was, with his essence, his soul. Coaching him became a joy. All work was done with aplomb. He was a star client.

REVIEW

We have discussed the importance of visualisation: dreaming your goal into reality. Tony reconnected with his soul and uncovered the 'right reasons' for his dreams and goals, through the power of visualisation. Now you can, too! I want you to think back to imagining your ideal life, and build on the connection to intuition you've worked on, in order to get really motivated about your dreams.

Visualising, or meditating to bring into focus and cement your ideas is the most powerful way to enlist the support of your soul, and fire up your motivation. By following and practising the following 'work' exercise, this process will become much easier. So, prepare to calm down, empty the mind of daily events, and chill . . .

THE WORK

1. Meditate. Sit in your comfiest chair, lie on your favourite rug – whatever; make yourself comfortable. Relax and close your eyes. Hear and feel your breathing: the air being drawn into your lungs, all the oxygen nourishing and energising the body, and then exhale. Each time you exhale, sense your body becoming more and more relaxed. With each breath you sink deeper and deeper into the chair, the bed, the carpet, and it feels good. Feel and then allow to relax each and every part of your body, beginning with your toes, then ankles, lower legs, and so on until you reach and relax the top of your head. Enjoy this relaxed state. Spend as long as you like getting there and then just remain there. Ten minutes minimum is a good starting point.

2. Imagine yourself again as the child you once were. Live the moment for as long as you want, then ask the child what they want to be when they grow up. Run the mental movie, let the child get excited and paint their picture.

3. Bring the movie up to date, and see yourself living your best life; the 'you' you were always meant to be. See it in detail; make the images in colour, super colour. Then add sound, smell and touch. Feel how good the sense of achievement is, the honesty and the absolute joy of life. Enjoy it. Smile. Celebrate it.

4. When you're ready begin to come back to the present. Gradually become aware of how your body feels in the room you're in right now, the temperature, your clothes. What noises can you hear? Sense your body, how it feels; your mind, how much more relaxed it is. Smile and slowly open your eyes, knowing the sight you've just seen is possible and accessible. It is the truth of who you really are, and with this knowledge from today you can make this dream a reality.

5. Now, write down the whole story. Taking your positivity journal, get going. Get excited. Make this story the best you've ever read – because this is *you*.

Key idea

Welcome to the new you!

5

Dealing with Gremlins

To live in the presence of great truths and eternal laws, to be led by permanent ideals – that is what keeps a man patient when the world ignores him, and calm and unspoiled when the world praises him

HONORÉ DE BALZAC

Getting motivated is about being aware and alert on many levels, but with one aim in mind: achieving your purpose. So far we have discussed beliefs, action planning, having a proactive approach, and making sure that our aspirations suit who we truly are. But what if after all that work we scupper our chances simply by tripping ourselves up? How many times have you really wanted to do something only to 'reason' yourself out of it even before taking the first step? Has there ever been an 'inner voice' telling you not to bother, it's not for you, you'll fail, everyone will laugh and be horrified by your actions? Ladies and gentlemen, may I introduce you, *for the very last time*, to your gremlin.

The aim of this chapter is to enable you to get rid of this little scoundrel. Imagine how much easier your life would be if you didn't have to contend with the stupid, unreasonable, unfounded, but powerful inner voice of doubt.

'But isn't *The Gremlins* a silly movie from the seventies?' I hear you ask. Well, yes, you're right, but the idea of gremlins is much older than that. In the movie, what began as a furry, cute little creature quickly developed into an overbearing monster with only one mindset: to cause havoc and destruction. In self-development work, the term 'gremlin' is used to describe those times when we doubt or second-guess ourselves, trip ourselves up, or blow our plans out of the water even before they've had a chance to swim.

Has this ever happened to you? Have you ever set yourself up to fail? By that, I mean even when you've had a plan or a dream, something has stopped you going for it 100 per cent. Why was that? Could it be because you believe it's just a waste of time, especially in a world where so many others will play 'all out' better than you – and win?

If this is your belief, guess what: you've got a case of the gremlins! By the end of this chapter I want you to be able to identify your own little voices of doubt, and recognise how they can trip you up and sabotage your very spark; then, even more importantly, I want you to have learned how to avoid them.

But first, we have to identify our gremlins. How do they manifest themselves in your world? Are they self-talk, or self-doubt? Recognising what they may say or suggest can be a very effective antidote against them. Below is a list of possible ways gremlins may make themselves heard. Please feel free to add your own. Recognition is the first step to eradicating them!

My gremlin says

- You can't do that
- You're a fool
- You're a failure
- Give in now before it's too late
- Nobody will believe you
- You're too big for your boots!
- I told you so

My gremlin makes me feel

- I failed
- I played small
- I didn't try hard enough
- It'll never happen
- I'm not as good as he/she is

I have met countless people who have told me they want to do this or that with their lives; to achieve a new career, relationship, or change the one they're in, to increase their wealth, or find themselves spiritually. We have a fabulously interesting conversation, by the end of which I'm as fired up by their plans as they are. Then, six months later, I run into them again and ask how they're getting on with the new life they spoke of so eloquently, and sadly I get a kind of stuttered, awkward silence, or, even worse, a list of excuses as to why it just didn't happen for them. Why do you imagine they have slipped? Does any of it sound familiar? I tell you: it's happened to me. In fact, I believe this scenario has happened to all of us to a greater or lesser degree.

So, what is it that stops us reaching our goal? Is it that we don't believe enough? It could be. Is it that our dream isn't formulated and solidified in our minds enough? Again, it could be. Might it even be that we have chosen the wrong vehicle to get us out of a situation we no longer want to be in? Again, this could be the case. But it's just as likely that we simply started to doubt ourselves. We second-guessed ourselves right out of the equation. We picked all the negatives rather than any positive, to such an extent that we became completely overwhelmed by our self-doubt. We listen to that little green man on our shoulder; you know, the one who tells you it'll all go wrong, you'll fail, you're stupid anyway, and that everyone will laugh and make fun of you. Ouch!

What can I say? Don't listen? Is that enough? Well, in short, yes. But if it were that easy none of us would suffer gremlins, and we'd all be super-duper successful, except we are not. So we have to be methodical: identify them systematically and then blow them well and truly out of the water.

It's as simple as that.

Gremlins can hit anybody, no matter how wealthy or seemingly successful. Super-achievers are just as likely to suffer attacks of self-doubt as anyone else. However, the one big difference between those who carry on and attain success, and those who give up, beaten and bruised, is simply their attitude and how they handle pangs of negativity; which is really just what a gremlin is. Take note here: a gremlin is not your intuition asking you to reconsider for the greater good. A gremlin is a negative little monster whose sole aim is to derail your life; end of story. So, step one to beating these little terrors is to be able to identify them.

Remember, it is your birthright to be able to achieve the life you want. There is nothing great about sitting back and letting life pass us by. We watch super-achievers – those in the arts, on the movie screen, in politics, medicine, or whatever field – lead full and amazing lives, and then we ask ourselves, 'Why not me?' Why *not* you? Unsupportive self-beliefs, self-doubt:

gremlins, that's why not you. Lack of solid self-confidence in yourself: that true and absolute 100 per cent belief in your dream is what is missing.

OUT OF FAILURE COMES SUCCESS

Those who fail big can still go on to enormous success. Imagine a person attempting to be the first to fly non-stop around the world in a hot-air balloon, but failing very publicly with a crash in the middle of the desert; and then trying, and failing spectacularly, yet again. Imagine a person trying to make the fastest sea crossing of the Atlantic, and having to be rescued from their wreck midway across. Imagine someone with the vision to try to buy Concorde from BA when the decision has been made to retire the whole fleet, but who is turned down. Despite these failures the person remains focused, their image untarnished, quite simply an enigma.

Of course, I am talking about Richard Branson, self-made multimillionaire businessman. How many times has that guy failed, and failed big? But we don't remember him for that. We remember his spirit in the face of failure. He smiles; is philosophical, and then gets straight back to his quest of pushing back the limits. He is a fabulous role model, demonstrating focus and determination while still upholding the principle of a decent human being.

Do you imagine Richard Branson sometimes has a

gremlin eating away at one of his new ideas? I'd stick my neck out and say almost certainly 'yes'. But do you think he pays it sufficient attention for it to knock his confidence so severely that the idea never gets off the ground? I doubt it very much.

That's what I want for you. To be able to identify any gremlins you may have, and then get rid of them one by one; and if in the future another one comes stumbling your way, you'll know what to do.

Ask yourself the following questions:

- Who am I when I'm feeling really happy?
- Who am I when I'm feeling sad?
- How do I see me?
- How do others see me?
- Are there any differences between the two?

It is a generally held belief that we have three selves: our true core self, our negative self, and the self we feel should be presented to other people. Ask yourself where the gremlin lives in you.

We have the potential to muddle our energies if our life doesn't fit the person we truly are, as well as the ability to sow the seeds of self-doubt, and encourage an attack of the gremlins. If we base our persona on who we imagine others would like us to be, or even who we feel we should be, rather than on who we really are then the rot sets in.

It is essential to know yourself more, and constantly be aware of how 'real' and 'true' you are.

But if you still do not feel 'real' or particularly connected with your inner self, then perhaps you have a gremlin. If so, don't feel daunted or overwhelmed; quite the contrary, be empowered. We are on our way; you are achieving a major shift in how you think about your life. Enjoy, and feel enormously proud of yourself.

AFFIRM SUCCESS

By creating and reciting a positive affirmation regularly you dramatically increase focus and the speed with which your plan will become reality. It has long been accepted by many cultures and faiths, such as Buddhism and Christianity, that repetitious chanting has positive effects. Whether affirmations bring us closer to our god, or closer to ourselves, their importance and usefulness remain. In self-development, the use of positive affirmations is proven to work, not least to blot out the detrimental effects of negative self-talk – gremlins! By following a few simple rules you too can increase the potency of whatever plan you have developed.

1. An affirmation must be stated in the present, as though what you want is already happening. No matter what your conscious mind is telling you, repeat your phrase in the present tense; for example, 'I will be hugely successful in my business,' would become, 'I *am* hugely successful in my business.' By expressing your affirmation in the future tense you're telling your subconscious mind that it hasn't happened yet, whereas by using the present tense you're convincing yourself that it already has.

2. Positive, positive, positive. Never say what you don't want, only what you do. Someone else may interpret, 'I don't want to have a fight with my boss at the meeting tomorrow,' as, 'I do want to have a fight with my boss at the meeting tomorrow' – and the person who interprets, or misinterprets, first may be you! Not a very good idea, right? So, with affirmations, as with all forms of communication (internal and external), get into the habit of only saying what you do want, not what you don't.

3. Give it emotion. That's right; by giving your affirmation emotional intensity you automatically increase its potency tenfold. For example, 'I love being hugely successful in my business,' sounds much better than the original in step 1. Equally, since now you have added feeling to your affirmation, remember to give it just that while you are saying or thinking it.

4. Make it physical. Even though it's great to recite your affirmation while, for example, meditating, imagine how much more powerful it would be to say it while out jogging, swimming, working out at the gym, running up stairs, walking the dog, even pushing the trolley round the supermarket!

5. Gremlin, what gremlin? Make your affirmation your new self-talk. From this moment on whenever the little green monster starts to whisper in your ear, recite your positive affirmation. The longer your gremlin talks, the longer you chant, the louder the gremlin moans, the louder you affirm the positive new you. Focus on the fact that there will be only one outcome to this encounter: you will win. You will win, and the gremlin? What gremlin? Precisely.

> Positive affirmations have many uses, all with the same objective: to move you forward. By using them to blot out the negative self-talk of a gremlin, not only do you remove one of the major obstacles to success, you also increase the focus of your mind towards your goal. Onwards, always onwards!

One word of warning. It's all very well to talk about gremlins, but what we are really talking about here is negative self-talk. And one critical piece of advice follows: *never* talk to your gremlin. Do not try to reason with yourself; simply by engaging in and opening a debate you've lost the battle. Don't go there. Just blot it out. Be positive. Focus. It is the only way. Commit to trying some of the affirmations below.

- I love the great new life I now have.

- I'm just so excited with the work I have as a (you fill it in) and deserve and enjoy all the success that comes my way as a result.

- I'm a terrific person who loves and enjoys life with loads of great friends.

- I'm just bubbling with life and enthusiasm.

- With my good health and positive energy I can change the world!

- I love myself, and know I'm a positive, energetic and fabulous person.

- I love being hugely successful in business.

KATIE'S STORY

Earlier this year I was coaching Katie, a beautiful, intelligent young lady who worked as cabin crew 'flying the flag' on one of the larger airlines. She loved her job and adored travelling. When at home she was incredibly busy taking study courses here, there and everywhere, a real scholar if ever I met one. The only trouble was she always felt shy and insecure around other people – not professionally, she was after all great at her job, but socially, one to one or in a group situation. She always felt as though she had nothing to say, or that if she opened her mouth no one would listen. Even at work, in personal interaction with other staff, she felt like a fish out of water.

I asked her to list her self-talk: phrases she said to herself or thought, and not stop until she got to at least fifty. When I'm coaching, I usually say to my clients, 'and don't stop until you get to at least fifty', and it always has the desired effect of horrifying them into action. The idea behind making such a huge list is that the first ten things are obvious, then up to twenty are things you only use from time to time, twenty to thirty are scraping the barrel, and then it gets interesting. From then on you're calling on the subconscious, raking things up from the depths of who you are. Fabulous.

There are two levels on which our gremlins can target us, the first being self-talk, the other self-belief. Both are important, but it is the second that is the more difficult to access and change. Horrendously long lists, while being stupidly long, and hence quite fun, are a great way of getting there in a hurry.

Classic negative self-talk

- I'm a klutz
- I'm stupid
- I'm forgetful/lazy/untidy
- I'm clumsy (and the list goes on . . .)

As well as looking at Katie's beliefs, and putting some positive and empowering new affirmations in place, we talked about literal conversation, by which I mean whatever she said to herself, how she referred to herself while talking to others, and most importantly what she *thought* about herself.

Although with me she expressed herself with ease on whatever topic we chose – and believe me we jumped around subjects with rapidity – in conversation with other people she just clammed up. Even after considerable time and effort, Katie still thought that she had nothing interesting to say. However, with a little practice and some brushing up of her general knowledge (reading a newspaper or a magazine, watching the news on television) so that she felt confident she did have something to say and perhaps even an opinion to express, she soon started to notice a change. Not only were people interested in her point of view, it was also fun. As with all action, once forward motion happens, it becomes self-propelling. For Katie, this was a new and fabulous experience.

Low self-esteem concerning day-to-day small talk is extremely common, and thankfully easily rectified. Whether you're a busy boffin or a hermit, if you never have time to read a newspaper, buy a glossy magazine, go to a football game, or even keep up to date with the soaps, can it be any wonder if after some time you find it a little difficult to 'connect' with the normal run of conversation – small talk? Get in the know. That's it. Do something, go somewhere, read something; be aware of what's happening in the world around you. It gives you something to say when you open your mouth, or when answering somebody else.

Ultimately, dealing with our gremlins is easy; living on a planet with 6 billion other people, and being the sociable creatures we intrinsically are, means we will begin a dialogue on some level outside ourselves. By identifying what's happening within, setting up a plan of action consistently to reduce and eradicate negative self-talk, while also increasing the amount of quality conversation we have with others we will make connections, and free ourselves of that old gripe, the gremlin.

THE WORK

1. Become aware of your gremlin, and then systematically disregard it. If it's pulling you down, belittling you, whatever, do the opposite of what it's saying.

2. Red lights. Write down a list of 'red-lighters', words or phrases your gremlin might use to unseat you and trip you up. Simply to bring them out in the open will deplete whatever power they have, while also reminding you what to look out for and avoid in the future.

3. Create a list of positive affirmations that work for you and could come to the rescue as and when you need them. Take a look at the list earlier in this chapter, and either use them or make up some new ones of your own. It's a great idea to use affirmations often; they really work.

4. Do something new today! Don't listen to gremlins that keep you fearful; take up a new hobby, learn Spanish, join a night class, have a head and shoulder massage, read a magazine you've never read before – and enjoy it. That's right, do something different, make the decision to have a good time, and follow through with it. Replacing the negative self-talk of a gremlin with a new, more positive vocabulary is always easier if you also occupy your senses with an exciting new activity.

5. Write a love letter to yourself. It's been said *so* many times that the person you should be able to love before anyone else is yourself, and it's true. Thankfully, and what is not usually expressed is that it's easy, easy, easy. Just make the decision to appreciate this amazing person you are.

Key Idea

You are more than who your gremlin says you are.

6

Putting It All Together

*Dost thou love life? Then do not squander time, for that is
the stuff that life is made of*

BENJAMIN FRANKLIN

The juggler mesmerises the crowd in the circus tent
with his skill. Two balls, three, four, five, all gliding
in perfect symmetrical orbit. Then come the hoops and
again every one of them seems to hang in the air at
the same time. He dances, weaves and curls, captivating
us all as he draws us into his fantastic, magical, beautiful new world – one of his making.

'Keeping all the balls in the air at the same time', has
become one of the most common phrases in the English
language today. It's often used in relation to business,
and more often than not goes hand in hand with copious
amounts of stress – otherwise there would be no need

to draw on the phrase at all, implying as it does that everything must be achieved 'at the same time'.

In life as a whole, our agenda is much broader. As you saw in chapter 2 with the Wheel of Life exercise, there are several, often competing areas in our lives, all vying for top place. But the various elements of our character go together to make up the amazing human being we are. Forget that, and you forget who you truly are and lose sight of your potential. If you disregard your whole self for too long, you may unleash a tidal wave that has the power to knock your life off kilter.

If, on the other hand, you can juggle, and juggle well, life will be joyous, a bed of roses. As Eddie and Debbie Shapiro wrote in their excellent book *Ultimate Relaxation*, personal power derives from a deep-seated, solid bond of friendship within ourselves, a self-knowledge that we accept and are happy with who we are.

WORK IN PROGRESS

I always refer to coaching and self-development as 'a work in progress', and I celebrate the fact, especially with my own journey of self-discovery. For many years now I have understood and welcomed that I will never know everything about the world, or indeed about myself. That basic fact is wonderful; it makes life worth living and a whole lot more fun besides. It means I'm always learning, and starting each day almost as a child – certainly one of the universe.

There will never be a time when life stands still and you have everything in order, balanced and 'in the air at the same time'. However, it is nonetheless crucial to have this as our objective, and I believe it is an excellent ideal since if we can balance the varying demands upon our time we keep the highest regard both for ourselves and those around us. In equilibrium we find our best chance of success, and that is our prize.

As you read this penultimate chapter, you should have a plan of action worked out, a route map of how to get from where you are now to where you want to be in life. You know how to crank up that motivation, how to check you're always in sync with your soul, even to watch out for the dreaded gremlins that seek to trip us up from time to time. Now begins the most beautiful and elegant technique of all: putting them all together into one flowing gesture.

OVER TO YOU

It's ironic, but the one thing a coach cannot do is the work on a client's behalf. Sure, we can talk about what should be done; we can motivate and rev someone up so that when they put down the phone they will go right ahead on the road to their own success. But at that point we leave the equation until the next week.

In the words of the old saying: 'We can take a horse to water, but we can't make it drink.'

This book aims to get you to the point where you'll put whatever part of your life that needs it into the required gear. I sincerely hope you've begun to act on your plans while reading this book, agreeing or disagreeing as the case may be, but moving forward nonetheless.

You see, what counts is the whole package of the dream, the plan, motivation, awareness and knowledge; how did that old song go? 'It's not what you do; it's the way that you do it – that's what gets results!' You better believe it. It's how you dress, how you present yourself, how you associate with people, and how you believe in yourself; how you methodically achieve and prove to yourself that you have indeed accomplished what you aimed to do on a daily basis. We're talking agenda; a scaling down of our dream into bite-sized pieces. Set yearly targets, half-yearly goals, weekly and then finally daily 'to do' lists that can be ticked off one by one so that two objectives can be met.

Firstly, you will become aware that achievements have been made, or, if not, you understand why not. Were expectations reasonable, well planned and reachable, or too high? At the end of each day, week or month, courses of action can be planned, readjusted and advanced based on previous results.

And secondly, you can take concrete steps: motivation

and self-confidence are interconnected and thrive as a result of reaching our stated objectives. We can build ourselves up along the way, using goal-setting, relaxation, motivational reading and affirmations, but only achievement will root these qualities in our psyche.

WAKE UP!

Or to put it a slightly different way: when you wake up each morning, ask yourself the following questions:

- What do I want from today?
- What kind of person do I need to be to achieve success?
- Who do I need to connect with today to help me move forward with life?
- Where would I meet a person like that?
- Why would they bother to talk to me? (What can I offer to their day?)
- What is my motivation for today?
- What is my self-talk (positive affirmation) of the day? (Recite it at least fifty times throughout the day *with feeling*!)

Maybe you particularly noticed two questions tucked away in the middle there: 'Who do I need to connect with today to help me move forward with life?' and 'What can I offer to their day?' I would suggest that our success depends largely on how well we choose to connect and work with our neighbours. 'Choose' because we do always have a choice – we determine our intention at the beginning of each and every day, hour and moment.

Why would any other person want to help us achieve our daily objectives? Generally, we attract others who are like us. People who look like us, talk like us, *act* like us, in the unspoken hope that we might somehow help them achieve what they need for success. It's a transaction, unspoken, even subconscious for the most part, until you realise it's also the best way to move ahead and achieve a better life.

So how do you act? Are you a tough business nut; sporty, easy-go-lucky, the 'smouldering' quiet type? How do you dress? Are you smartly suited, chinos, chintz, sex god/goddess, or Oxfam chic? Opposites sometimes do attract, after a lot of hard work, but mostly we attract others who are like us. It's easier. If your game plan involves an image or whole life upgrade, be certain to think out properly where you're going and how you'll get there. Make sure you attract people into your life who you would choose, as, possibly unknowingly, they will help you make your life work.

SETTING OUT YOUR STALL

It's 'sort out our agenda' time! What do you need to

improve about You, plc? You already have the plan and steps worked out by now, so this is the moment to put it all into practice. When was the last time you gave yourself a 'life MOT'? Most of us love our cars, and even though they may be running fantastically well, I'm sure none of us would just take that for granted year in year out, would we? And once the car reaches a certain age it has to have an MOT, to see that all is well and it is still roadworthy. We carry out a service on any parts that need upgrading. We regularly clean, polish, vacuum, deodorise and buy nice new carpets to put our feet on while driving: the list is endless – so many tasks we undertake willingly, all for the love of our car! You're getting my drift here: just because our car is new and perfect doesn't mean we don't take care of it.

But what about ourselves? Messy haircuts, mis-matched socks, old jeans, smelly jackets, yellow teeth? Yuk! As I said, it's a 'life MOT' moment. With all the tools you've learned to use to move your life forward, you should find this easy, and you owe it to yourself. Begin today.

SONIA'S STORY

Born in the Czech Republic and moving to England, the country of her dreams, some ten years ago, when Sonia came to me she was outwardly successful, both financially and professionally. A graduate of the London School of Economics, she had worked as a merchandiser with several of the larger companies in the UK, and had the air of a nice, friendly and successful young woman. I asked her what she wanted out of coaching. 'Order,' was her response. She had achieved the life she wanted in London for so many years, but at a price, that of her wellbeing; she was frayed at the edges.

Sonia was outwardly in control; inwardly waiting for everything to fall apart, wondering how much longer she could 'keep all the balls in the air at the same time'. She described her life as one big whirl. Just listening to an account of a week in Sonia's life made me feel tired.

She already used her diary carefully; each day was packed to its limit. So I asked about her *intention* with each new day: what did she want to achieve from it and how would she know if it had been a success or not? She did not have an answer. We both realised that in her haste to survive and 'make her mark' on the world, she had somehow lost her way. She performed one unconnected task after another, their only link being that she was doing it. I asked if she thought her life fitted with who she now was, or who she ultimately wanted to be. I got a negative on both counts.

> *Hold on to your dreams for they are, in a sense,*
> *the stuff of which reality is made. It is through our*
> *dreams that we maintain the possibility of a*
> *better, more meaningful life*
>
> **LEO BUSCAGLIA**

This chapter aims to beg the fundamental question: What is your motivation? What is your motivation for wanting to make life work better for you than perhaps it already does? What do you want to change or create in your life and why? I ask all my private coaching clients this question, usually more than once: first certainly at the beginning, but then after a couple of months – when they're least expecting it. The *why* is probably the most important part of all; it's the glue that will stick everything else together.

In the first instance it's good to know if what you're doing is 'from the heart', which can sound a little precious, I know, but, especially following the last couple of chapters, with real honesty it shouldn't. I support clients to the hilt, but if they're seeking approval from me then they're looking in the wrong place. The justification and reason for upgrading should come entirely from you.

When Sonia became aware, for the first time, why she had created the life she now lived, it was a real eye-opener. Sure, she had had the initial reason when she arrived from the Czech Republic, and no doubt subconsciously at times since (university, job hunting and so on), but for the most part life was busy; it just happened for her.

Putting a new vision in place became a labour of love in itself. Sonia really adored her life. Nothing needed to change drastically: just a tweak here and there, a deeper appreciation, was all that was needed.

Six months later we spoke for the last time. Sonia was still as friendly and lovely as ever, but with a relaxed, softer, quietly vivacious manner that certainly hadn't been there before. Everything fitted in, and time was still utilised to its fullest. But being busy just for the sake of it had long gone. Relaxation, friends, a social life, pampering time was now scheduled in. Why? Because she deserved it. This cool new persona was Sonia's way of rewarding herself for all the hard work and occasional long hours that were now an even more important part of her life. She had looked at her job with a detached eye, and come to the conclusion she loved it!

I'm sure at some point Sonia will think to 'touch base' and tell me how she's getting on. But I know she'll be fine. Her energy rose several notches just by becoming aware of what was happening with her life, and what she needed to do to improve its overall quality. In short, Sonia did a 'life MOT'.

THE GAME PLAN

Ask yourself the following questions:

- How will I use this knowledge I've learned?
- What specific plans and ideas will I utilise?
- How will it prove useful, in the short term and long term?
- What will all this work enable me to do?
- What is the most immediate thing I can achieve right now?

Bring in the cavalry, your support structure! That's right, don't try to change the world or even *your* world all by yourself. Everyone needs support sometimes. Be systematic about it; rather than waiting and hoping it'll happen, make it happen.

By support structure, I mean things you've put in place to help you to take the strain – in good times as well as bad. Just by having a written plan of action that you can call upon to realign and centre yourself, you have support. By listing all the reasons for aiming for your dream you're creating further support. By affirming your very goodness, your intent, your 'finished article', you're setting in place what will keep you strong.

Outwardly, it is vital to be wise and selective as to those who surround you and with whom you share your dream. Also, a list of one or two good people who will not mollycoddle or criticise you when you need a friendly voice is an absolute must at the end of a long, hard day.

I have such a list in the back of my diary. In tougher times we do not always think so logically as to who or what to call upon, so I chose an easy place where I know I'll remember to look in an emergency (in more tranquil moments, I know these contacts without needing to look at a list).

Lastly, I have 'fun' things to lighten my stress, mood, or whatever. They include going to see a really funny comedy movie, live cabaret (especially comedy), going to the gym, the park, jogging, and of course reading an inspirational book.

I know from experience that any one of the above will lighten my load. What is it for you? A support structure is essential at any time, and so to put one in place while reassessing more general life plans seems just the most natural thing to do.

THEN DO IT!

From time to time I find it useful to set out in black and white (remember the 3 per cent study?) everything that is happening in my life. Indeed, since life is always a 'work in progress', sands shift and new opportunities come along. Without taking stock and being aware, by means of a 'life MOT' two or three times a year, how can we complain if a chance here or fresh opportunities there passes us by unnoticed?

Use the following template to make your own list of values, rating each out of a possible ten. First think back to how you felt before starting this book, followed by today, and then return at prearranged times in the future (use your diary to schedule these) to be aware of what's happening and changing. Knowledge is power, and self-knowledge is the most powerful of all.

I've provided an example here but, remember, my values (as listed) may not be yours, so delete and fill in your own as needed.

Prioritise values (example)	When started book	Today	1 Week	1 Month	3 Months
Independence					
Self-development					
Honesty (self)					
Drive					
Determination					

Prioritise values (example) *(Cont'd)*	When started book	Today	1 Week	1 Month	3 Months
Friends/others					
Plan (order)					
Time-keeping					
Risk-taking					

It is worth saying that time-keeping means utilising time in the best way possible on any given occasion (e.g. work, play, study), and risk-taking is with regard to stepping up to the podium of self-development. Simply doing things differently, questioning the status quo, being willing to take a step into the unknown constitute taking risks – all power to you if that's what you've decided to do.

Stepping into the unknown and taking risks in life has its own rewards, not least the obvious ones of possible success. The most amazing is one of the laws of the universe: by giving out, by putting your life in its most natural gear, the universe tends to reward you by handing back a way, a route to success. It does work.

When finally you swim with your own natural current, things will happen.

THE WORK

1. Recheck your Wheel of Life. Work with it. See where you are now and how much you've moved in this short time. Break down and combine into chunks all the various tasks you decided upon in your daily schedule, and then be diligent in completing what you set out to achieve.

2. Stay in touch with your soul; does what you've now embarked upon still 'feel' right? Refer back to the exercises in chapter 4, and above all be honest with your heart. If you've moved off course, barked up the wrong tree, or just plain changed your mind about what you want to do, be brave enough to stop, reassess and start again. This is your life in action: always remember, unique as it is, it is simply a 'work in progress'.

3. Stay positive. The moment you start doubting yourself, telling yourself you should give up, *stop* and take action to shut that nasty little gremlin up! Need I say more? I think not.

4. Commit to taking at least one positive action per day – whether it be phoning someone listed on your support structure, developing your ideal life, or doing the hardest of your daily tasks *first* – so that you know you're serious, and moving in the right direction: forward!

5. Juggle! Have fun with all of the above. Mix it up, make mistakes, get successful – but put it all into action. How many balls can you keep in the air at the same time? Make your life magnificent; enthral all who come into contact with you. Juggle.

Key Idea

Life is only as strong as its weakest link.

7

Enjoying the Journey

All successful men and women are big dreamers. They imagine what their future could be, ideal in every respect, and then they work every day toward their distant vision, that goal or purpose

BRIAN TRACY

So, here we are at the end of my little book of ideas designed to get you moving, get you contemplating new strategies – 'thinking out of the box' – and get you motivated to create a better life. Isn't that what it's all about? There is the story of the man, old and grey, sitting in his rocking chair, looking back over his life. He had kept focused, promising himself such a reward when he achieved the success he strived for. The funny thing was that now, from his rocking chair, he could see so many times when he had achieved that kind of success: in a friendship, a smile, a business deal, his home, family, when he scored that goal, when he held his son, felt the joy of loving his wife. But he'd never stopped long enough to realise that before, and even though now of course was not too late, it did seem a shame he'd never thought to celebrate before.

What would you celebrate right now? What would be ten reasons for you to smile, feel happy, with a sense of joy and achievement in your heart, that you had achieved something worthwhile, something good in your life? Because I want you to stop here and celebrate. Begin what you mean to carry on. Life is not just a journey of progress and accomplishment, but also one of celebration and gratitude for . . . and you fill in the blanks.

How would it be if, at the beginning of each day, you ran through a spontaneous list of all you were grateful for? Spoken aloud or quietly within the mind, a list of acknowledgement for all that is good and positive in your life.

And how would it be if, at the end of the day, you again made a spontaneous list of all that was good for you, all that was nurturing for you, all that you were grateful for – and let that be your last thought as you drifted off to sleep? Imagine, no more counting sheep to drop off to sleep, but listing positives and gratitude? It would be amazing.

Setting up these new habits is important, and will serve you well in life. Especially at the beginning, assignments that remind you to acknowledge and respect yourself, others, and all the great situations and moments in your life is a good ongoing *work in progress*, and might include . . . (Following are some suggestions collected from many clients throughout the years. Feel free to borrow from, enjoy or develop your own. The important thing is to enjoy the process.)

- Run through all the things you're grateful for at least twice per day (best is first thing in the morning and last thing at night)
- Appreciate why you're such an amazing human being
- Smile at least twenty times per day
- Say 'hello' to at least three strangers each day
- Forgive yourself consciously at least once per day
- Ask three people how they are, and really listen to the answers!
- Spend ten minutes looking at yourself in the mirror, getting to know and appreciate all the lines, colours, textures and individualities of your face – and loving it!
- Look into somebody's eye, say, 'Thank you', and mean it
- Say a prayer, to say 'thank you', and that you love you, to yourself (whatever your religion)

THE JOURNEY IS AS IMPORTANT AS THE DESTINATION

Deepak Chopra, in his book *The Path to Love*, explains how we will never follow a path for long if it is not natural for us. We have to be 'doing the right thing', or else it'll just be an uphill struggle, hard work, or simply won't work out at all.

It is our journey that will be the true enjoyment. I'm sure we have all read or heard about people who spent their whole lives looking, working towards something they couldn't quite put their finger on. Enjoyment was suspended for the duration, or until they reached that summit of success. Except in their eyes success was never quite achieved. They grew old, and only realised at the very end of their lives that it was the journey that had been the real success. They had lived their entire lives with an aim, an objective in mind. Successful planning and diligent work had been accomplished over many years, yet none of it had been noticed, acknowledged, or, most importantly, rewarded.

I began this book with my belief that self-development should be seen as a 'work in progress'. The very nature of what you've embarked upon should excite and enthral you. By the end of this chapter I want you to have begun your very own self-development, which will enable you to reassess your progress and your levels of motivation consistently, on the way to making life better.

To complete this chapter here are some more techniques to keep you 'on the right road' – *your* road to your ideal life.

LIVE WITH PASSION

It's a cliché, I know, but true nonetheless. No matter what you do, do it as if you mean it – with passion. What would be the point of living a kind of 'half life' of wanting to do something, but constantly pussy-footing around it? No one would do that, would they? I remember one person who did for many years: me. It wasn't until I was in my twenties that I could find the courage to move to London to pursue my dream of working in performance. When I did, I was finally able to love my life, live it passionately and reap the rewards that came my way as a result.

Susan Jeffers took the bull by the horns with her groundbreaking book *Feel the Fear, and Do It Anyway*. The title really does say it all, and yet with such a calm, self-effacing manner about her, Susan does not come over at all 'in your face' or aggressive. Hers is the gentle, natural way: the path of true love. This love is the one we should all feel for ourselves. Because out of it comes respect for, and belief in the infinite goodness of who we are. With that, we can achieve anything.

TWO OPPOSITES

Howard Hughes and David Beckham, while not only from different generations, had directly opposite experiences of the place they allowed success in their lives. First, Howard Hughes, born 24 December 1905. He quickly found fame and fortune as a billionaire industrialist, film producer, film director and aviator, but by his fifties had become a super-rich recluse, travelling the world shrouded in darkened hotel rooms, hiding away from the fame and celebrity he had created.

Does his story suggest happiness and connectivity, enjoyment of his journey? I think not.

David Beckham, on the other hand, relishes and is vibrant within his unique life. He knows the trade-off of his immense wealth and success is to exist in a goldfish bowl of media attention. Long ago, he and wife, Victoria, decided that fame was a price worth paying for the level of success they sought.

David is not only an extraordinarily gifted football player, fashion icon and media figure, he also *looks* completely at peace with who he is. He's enjoying his life. That's what sets him apart from most other wannabe personalities, hungry and aggressive for more. David, however, for all the media intrusion and scrutiny way past what most would describe as normal, just smiles, entertained that anyone would be interested in him at all, and happy with his status.

GLORIA'S STORY

'I don't know what to do any more. I've brought up the kids, been a good mum, but what now? I know I've got something else to give, but feel lost if you really want to know.' That was Gloria's description of herself the first time we spoke. She didn't call me because she felt powerful beyond measure, she hadn't got a high-flying career and wanted more: more focus, more social life, more success. Gloria wanted a life.

At forty-two with four children she felt she had reached her point of no return. Her youngest child was now in high school; Gloria worked in the admin section of a large department store. She was a mother, wife, colleague, friend, neighbour – the list went on. Missing from the list was who Gloria was for herself.

Many women lose their identity during the 'mothering' years – for the most admirable of reasons – but as time moves on recovering awareness of who you are and what you need to survive is important; otherwise there may come a day when you suddenly feel 'lost' and don't know what to do about it. Men can also experience the same feeling, most noticeably when leaving work as a result of redundancy or retirement. Re-establishing and reassessing who we are can be seen as an opportunity rather than a crisis; again it's our choice.

Our busy lives can make us forget to relish each day for what it is. 'The other man's grass is always greener' scenario can on the one hand inspire and motivate us, but it can also blind us to the joy and abundance we already have in our journey through life.

I asked Gloria what was good about her present situation and her immediate reaction was that she was completely stumped for anything to say. Of course, she loved her children and husband, liked her colleagues and her job, and . . . and slowly as she told me what was good, it began to dawn on her what a blessed life she already had. Her 'things I'm grateful for' list ran to several pages and at the end of our coaching remained one of the watershed moments for her. Finally, she realised she didn't live a 'little' life at all; in fact it was huge and amazing – she'd just forgotten to stop long enough to recognise it as such.

What could you be grateful for in your life today? A follow-on to that list, and again one Gloria enjoyed, was 'things I love about my journey are . . .' What do you love about your life journey? I'm not saying ignore the tough stuff and deny the challenges, but let's just redress the balance – beginning today. 'Things I love about my journey are . . .'

The nub of it with Gloria was that she'd always wanted to become a writer. She'd never had anything published, but had written lots of short stories and articles just for herself through the years. After only a little encouragement she enrolled in an evening creative writing class, which she instantly loved. For her, it was as much about connecting with others of the same mind as about writing. She was living her journey, instead of subconsciously waiting for it to be over.

Once she found her focus, while still doing the admin job forty hours per week, not to mention raising her family, being a good mother as well as a dutiful wife, everything was possible. She would even take a floppy disk to work so that she could do some writing as she ate her lunch!

A year later and Gloria has finished her first novel – oh, didn't I mention she got herself a book deal? She did. Wow! Even now, when people I work with get focused and make their world move I stand back in awe. It's fabulous. When you connect with your world, and not just the destination, the world connects with you and you just hang on for the ride!

GOOD NEWS

Deal in good news. Surround yourself with positivity. From this moment on make a concerted effort to filter out all the bad stuff. Be aware of negative energy; it comes in many and varied forms. You have decided to upgrade who you are, to achieve your full potential, to make life work. So give it all the goodness you possibly can.

INFLUENCES

You've become aware of the many and differing areas of your life today; now there is one more to dig out of the closet and set in order: influences.

A. Positive Influences In My Life?	B. Negative Influences In My Life?
Successful partner	Watching the news too often
Supportive and successful friends and colleagues: Carrie Jane George JJ	Too many soap operas People (list, and why) Reading only the bad/ sensational news in newspapers
Inspirational books *Be Your Own Life Coach* *The 7 Habits of Highly Effective People* *Take Charge of Your Life*	Too much alcohol Unfit Lack of sleep Horror and other scary movies
Biographies	
Positive magazines Positive role models (those we aspire to emulate)	

As you can see from my list of examples, I have a much longer list of positives than negatives – that is your objective. Don't worry if at the moment your negatives far outweigh the positives; the first step is simply to become aware. But, of course, once you are aware it's going to be more difficult to disregard what you have written and is staring you in the face. That's great. That alone will act as an incentive for you to alter the balance.

From this day on I want you to remove negative influences from your life, and replace them with more and more positives, step by step. The larger this first column becomes, the stronger you get, and the more able you will be to repel any future onslaughts – including the gremlin kind. So, fill in the lists on the following page; and be totally honest with yourself.

A. Positive Influences In My Life?	B. Negative Influences In My Life?

Make it your life's work to overload yourself with positive influences. You are also creating another visual reminder of what your support structure looks like. All the positives can be called upon to inspire or support, calm and generate more positivity in the times when we don't perhaps feel so productive or happy with our world. Those are the times when we need especially to remember to call on our support structure.

DREAM BIG!

That's right, never dream small. Don't get shy with what you're thinking, for they are your thoughts and no one else's. Dream is what a child does quite naturally; however as we grow up it's knocked, educated, or 'reasoned' out of us. Along with intuition, dreaming is one of our most valuable, God-given assets and, as with any other skill, we either use it or lose it.

So, from today I want you to include all your most positive dreams in your positivity journal. I'm not suggesting you try to remember every detail of your dream last night. No, what I mean is that you take the positive self-talk we all have and record it for use now or in the future. Get those dreams down on paper!

Recording dreams and moments of inspiration can provide a commentary, a kind of soundtrack to your life; by writing, reading and constantly adding to and working from these thoughts, they live. Your journey becomes less of an uphill slog, and more of a joy, an exciting journey towards a better tomorrow.

FINAL CHECKLIST

- What would I do if I knew I couldn't fail?
- What is stopping me right now from simply going for it?
- What is it costing me not to go for it?
- What will making the decision to act bring to my life today?
- How can I support myself today, tomorrow, next week?
- What will my life look like six months from now?
- How good will it make me feel to go for this dream?
- How do I feel, out of ten (ten being high), about making this decision?

CLOSING THOUGHTS

It is clear that one of the major factors determining whether we feel we are having a rewarding, enjoyable and worthwhile life is our level of motivation. Getting motivated is our ticket to a better life. More than anything else, it is not so much what life throws at us, so much as how we handle and shape it to the best of our ability that will define who we are. Motivation is having a thirst for life, and if this book has helped you on the road to rediscovering or finding yours, then we have achieved a great success.

THE WORK

1. Get excited about life! That's right, take a step back and realise what an amazing life you have. With all the work you've been doing in this book you should already be there and feeling great. If, however, you're not there yet, ask yourself if what is happening in your world is what you really want. If you need to, reread chapter 4, 'Accessing the Soul'.

2. Have a party! Celebrate all that is now happening in your life. If you feel supported by those you know, then fabulous, tell them of your dreams and draw them into your web of success. However, if you're not too sure you want to say anything yet, or equally not convinced your friends will be the right ones for the duration, then keep shtoom, and have a party anyway, just for the fun of it. Remember, the party is your state of mind, the celebration that now you are on course, getting motivated!

3. Plan ahead. Make planning ahead fun, something you look forward to, as much a part of your week as having your nails done or going to the gym. This is your time, and it doesn't have to take hours of sweat, just ten to fifteen minutes at the end of each day. The secret is to integrate it into your routine in a way that feels right.

4. Get ready for success, read up on it, research and put together a scrap book of cuttings, pictures and writing of the life you want to create for yourself.

It's quite likely that someone, somewhere has already achieved a dream similar to yours, and that in itself can be used to the good. It gives you someone to emulate, to learn from; and the opportunity to study how they did it. Of course, your achievement will be unique, because your responses, feelings, values and a whole myriad of attributes are simply and only you.

5. Always look forward. It is said that most people give up on their dreams when success is only one step away. Of course, at that time they do not realise it. But for those who do carry on, they know this is true. Once you find your true purpose, if you know deep down in your heart that this path is the one you were meant to follow, do not let anyone or anything blow you off course.

If sometimes life gets tough and makes you doubt yourself, use all that I have talked about in these pages, find all the other books that can support you, reread your positivity journal, meditate, take action, call upon your support structure, and above all: *do not give up!*

I wish you all the very best in your quest to 'Get Motivated'. Please drop me a line at any time and tell me how you're getting on: my address is *info@mike blissett.com* (or via *www.fionaharrold.com*).

Key Idea

Your life is a perfect work of art; paint it with all the colour and light that you are.

Transform your life
with Hodder Mobius

For the latest information on the best in
Spirituality, Self-Help,
Health & Wellbeing and Parenting,

visit our website
www.hoddermobius.com

Have a conversation without words ; explore body language.

play chinese whispers.

conversation openers.
endings conversations.
joining a conversation late.

pass the sentence —
everyone writes a sentence
then folds it over & passes
it on — 'play music' during
this exercise.

Treasure chest —
put in it — skills & strengths,
what they like about themselves,
achievements.

'Toolkit' — what is your

Reveal in g yourself.
Taking care of yourself
Doing something interesting
  stimulating your brain.
Taking on new challenges.

role - play.

settling an argument.

Interview questionnaire
what makes a good friend!
  " " " good relationships.

Having 1 instead of general
Use open-ended questions.
play the yes/no game.